SIX FIGURES AHEAD:

Revealing the Subsequent Measures for Monetary Achievement

JANE O. GOLD

Copyright 2024, by JANE O. GOLD. All rights reserved.

This document may not be replicated or reproduced in any form without permission from the publisher.
Moreover, the information inside cannot be transferred, stored electronically, or maintained in a database.

And the document cannot be copied, scanned, fixed, or kept in its entirety without the publisher's or creator's consent.

TABLE OF CONTENTS

TABLE OF CONTENTS 5
INTRODUCTION 7
CHAPTER ONE 9
   RECOGNIZING YOUR PRESENT FINANCIAL SITUATION 9
CHAPTER TWO 17
   DEVELOPING A WEALTH-MINDSET 17
CHAPTER THREE 27
   CREATING SEVERAL REVENUE SOURCES 27
CHAPTER FOUR 35
   EXAMINING VARIOUS REVENUE SOURCES: CHARTING THE COURSE FOR ECONOMIC INDEPENDENCE 35
CHAPTER FIVE 41
   TECHNIQUES FOR INCREASING YOUR INCOME 41
CHAPTER SIX 53
   EFFECTIVE BUDGETING AND SAVINGS STRATEGIES: ESTABLISHING A STRONG FINANCIAL BASE 53
CHAPTER SEVEN 57
   THE BUDGETING BLUEPRINT: A PATHWAY TO ECONOMIC INDEPENDENCE 57
CHAPTER EIGHT 63
   TAKING ADVANTAGE OF AUTOMATED SAVINGS: A ROUTE TO MONETARY INDEPENDENCE 63

CHAPTER NINE 67
  JUDICIOUS INVESTING FOR SUSTAINABLE GROWTH 67
CHAPTER TEN 71
CONCLUSSION 75
  FINAL THOUGHTS: REACHING SIX FIGURES AND BEYOND 75

INTRODUCTION

Welcome to "Six Figures Ahead: Revealing the Subsequent Measures for Monetary Achievement"! Have you ever happened to think about what your bank account might look like with six figures? Among the many advantages that accompany accomplishing that desired goal are a feeling of stability, the liberty to follow your passions, and the assurance that you can support your loved ones without question.

As much as we all want to, the reality is that many of us view reaching six figures as an unattainable goal that belongs to a select few or involves winning the lottery. I am here to tell you, though, that it is completely achievable, and this book will outline the precise steps to take you there.

In "Six Figures Ahead," we're not just discussing reaching a financial goal and hanging up the phone. Instead, we're delving deeply into the actions you must take to genuinely safeguard your financial future—the methods, attitude adjustments, and strategies.

To begin with, we will assist you in comprehending your existing financial situation. Where are you at this moment? What are your sources of income, assets, and debts? Having a clearer understanding of your financial status will help you make more informed decisions going forward.

But that's only the start. We'll also look at the wealth mindset—the attitudes, routines, and convictions that set wealthy people apart from others. You'll discover how to develop a prosperity mindset that draws opportunities and wealth into your life.

After that, we'll go into the doable tactics for creating several revenue sources. Creating digital products, investing in real estate, or launching a side business are just a few of the income-generating options you'll learn about that can help you reach your financial objectives sooner than you ever imagined.

However, we won't stop there. Additionally, we'll demonstrate how to use passive income streams to build long-term wealth and financial independence. Doesn't it sound too wonderful to be true to wake up to money that has been transferred into your bank account while you slept? It's not, and we'll walk you through the process step-by-step.

Therefore, if you're prepared to take charge of your financial destiny, to overcome the constraints imposed by your existing salary, and to begin creating the life you've always wanted, then get ready to embark on an endless journey that will lead you to six figures.

CHAPTER ONE
RECOGNIZING YOUR PRESENT FINANCIAL SITUATION

Prior to creating a plan to achieve six-figure success, we must first recognize our current situation. We'll dig deep into your current financial situation in this chapter, looking at your assets, debts, sources of income, and spending.

Before you can take any significant steps toward your goals, you must have a clear grasp of your financial status. This entails assessing your liabilities, which include debts and other financial commitments, in addition to your assets, which include savings, investments, and real estate.

With a clearer understanding of your existing financial status, you'll be better able to pinpoint problem areas and create a strategy for reaching your financial objectives. This could entail reducing spending, raising your income, or paying off debt.

However, comprehending your financial situation involves more than just doing the math; it also entails learning about your spending patterns, attitudes, and convictions. Do you prone to overspend and live beyond your means, or are you someone who saves and invests carefully? Do you think in terms of abundance and opportunity, or do you think in terms of scarcity?
Through an honest and transparent assessment of your financial situation, you can learn a great deal about your

strengths and shortcomings as a money manager. Your route to six-figure success will be built on this awareness, which will enable you to make wise decisions and take significant action to achieve your objectives.

There is a landscape as varied and active in the enormous field of personal finance as there is in the outside world. We all walk this terrain, but it's still quite mysterious and uncertain to many. where we will set out on an exploration to comprehend the nuances of your financial environment.

Introducing Blossom, a recent college graduate with big plans and aspirations for the future. Blossom, like many young adults, is ready to forge her own path in life as she stands on the brink of maturity. But in the middle of all the excitement and anticipation, Blossom is forced to face a difficult truth: she needs to comprehend her financial situation.

However, what does it really mean to comprehend your financial environment? Fundamentally, it's about getting a comprehensive picture of your financial status, including assets and liabilities in addition to income and expenses. The idea is to assess your current situation and set goals for the future by taking stock of where you are now.

For Blossom, the first step in her journey is a straightforward assessment of her financial status. With a pen and paper in hand, she starts to list all of her sources of income, including her entry-level employment and the occasional freelancing contract. After that, she focuses on her spending, carefully cataloging all of her out-of-pocket costs, including groceries, entertainment, and utilities as well as rent.

Blossom realizes how dire things are when she looks at her financial condition. Her salary is insufficient to meet her expenses, even with her best efforts, leaving little space for saves or investments. Though depressing, this insight acts as a spark for improvement.

However, comprehending your financial situation is more than just doing the math; it also involves learning about your spending patterns, mindset, and actions. Blossom has to examine her spending habits closely in order to pinpoint areas where she may make savings and cut back.

She starts to notice trends as she thinks back on her spending behaviors. She acknowledges that she often overspends on impulsive purchases, whether it's a last-minute weekend trip or the newest technology. Her long-term financial objectives are being severely harmed by this practice, which is simple to defend in the heat of the moment.

Blossom's adventure doesn't stop there, though. Realizing how outside influences shape your financial reality is another aspect of understanding your financial environment. Numerous factors might affect your financial well-being, ranging from market volatility and economic trends to cultural influences and society conventions.

For Blossom, this entails accepting the difficulties of residing in a world that is becoming more unstable and uncertain. Her path is paved with challenges, from the escalating expense of living to the unpredictability of the labor market. But now that she has a clearer grasp of her financial situation, Blossom is more prepared to face and conquer these obstacles.

Realizing that your financial situation is dynamic and always changing as a result of external factors is possibly the most crucial part of knowing your financial landscape. Something that is true now might not be true tomorrow, thus it's critical to modify and alter as necessary.

This entails adopting a resilient and adaptable mindset for Blossom. It entails having the flexibility to change directions and stay on course when required while pursuing her financial objectives with unwavering determination. She will find great use for this lesson as she pursues her goal of six figures in revenue.

With a renewed feeling of purpose and clarity, Blossom closes the chapter on her investigation of her financial environment. She has plotted her path and set sail for a better financial future, so she is no longer lost in a sea of uncertainty.

Set out on your own path of exploration. Give yourself enough time to comprehend your financial situation, including where you are now and where you hope to be in the future. You can only set out on the path to the abundant and prosperous life you deserve by developing a greater grasp of your financial situation.

Understanding your present financial status is a crucial first step in taking charge of your money and achieving your financial objectives. It entails obtaining data regarding your earnings, outlays, possessions, and debts in order to obtain a thorough grasp of your financial situation. This is a thorough how-to guide for determining your present financial situation:

1. Collect Financial paperwork: To begin, gather all pertinent financial records you possess, such as bank statements, credit card statements, investment statements, pay stubs, loan paperwork, and any other supporting documentation. Accurately assessing your financial condition will be made easier if you have these documents on hand.

2. Calculate Your Income: Find out how much money you make overall from all sources, such as rental income, commissions, bonuses, wages, and any other income you may have from investments or salaries. A longer term average will provide a more realistic picture if your income fluctuates from month to month.

3. Explain What You Spent: List every item you incur each month in great detail, dividing it up into fixed and variable categories (e.g., groceries, dining out, entertainment) and fixed (e.g., rent or mortgage, utilities, utilities). Remember to factor in unpredictable or sporadic expenses, such as yearly maintenance fees or subscriptions.

4. Examine Your Spending Patterns: Examine your spending patterns to find areas where you might be overpaying or where you might be able to make savings. Examine your spending for any patterns or trends, and decide if there are more affordable options or if some expenses are really required.

5. Calculate Your Net Worth: Take your entire assets less your total liabilities (debts) to find your net worth. Cash, investments, real estate, cars, and other valuables are examples of assets; debts such as credit card debt, mortgages, school loans, and other outstanding loans are examples of liabilities.

6.Check Your Credit Report: Get a copy of your credit report from Equifax, Experian, and TransUnion, the three main credit bureaus, and carefully go over it to look for any mistakes or inconsistencies. Information from your credit report, which can impact your overall financial health, is useful in determining your credit history, amount of outstanding obligations, and payment history.

Examine your emergency fund and savings. You can find out if you have enough saved for emergencies or unforeseen costs by reviewing your emergency fund and savings accounts. To be prepared for unforeseen financial difficulties, you should ideally have three to six months' worth of living expenses saved in an accessible account.

8.Assess Your Money Objectives: Contemplate your immediate and future financial objectives, including home ownership, retirement savings, debt repayment, and company startup. Determine whether these objectives are in line with your existing financial condition and what modifications or alterations you might need to make to get there.

9.Seek Professional Advice if Needed: You should think about consulting a financial advisor or planner if you're unclear of how to evaluate your financial status or if you require assistance creating a financial strategy. Experts can offer tailored advice based on your unique situation and assist you in developing a plan for reaching your financial objectives.

10. Regularly Review and Update Your Financial Situation: Lastly, keep in mind that fluctuations in income, expenses, market circumstances, or life events can all cause your financial situation to alter over time. Develop the routine of periodically reviewing and updating your financial status to make sure you're staying on course to meet your objectives and to make any required corrections afterward.

Through adherence to these guidelines and a proactive evaluation of your existing financial circumstances, you can acquire significant understanding of your financial well-being, pinpoint opportunities for enhancement, and embark on a journey towards elevated financial prosperity and stability.

CHAPTER TWO
DEVELOPING A WEALTH-MINDSET

It's time to focus on the wealth mindset after you have a clearer understanding of your present financial situation. This chapter will demonstrate why, as they say, "wealth is 90% mindset and 10% mechanics."

The foundation of the wealthy mindset is developing an empowered and positive relationship with money. It's about adopting an attitude of abundance and possibility instead of one of scarcity and limitation. Regardless of your current situation, it's about having faith in your potential to produce prosperity and abundance in your life.

However, it's not as simple as it sounds to develop a wealth attitude. In order to achieve this, one must be self-aware, introspective, and willing to question ingrained attitudes and ideas regarding money. It entails facing your money-related worries and fears head-on and putting confidence and optimism in their place.

We will examine several typical money mindset fallacies and provide strategies for escaping them. In-depth discussions of the benefits of abundance thinking and thankfulness will be covered, along with techniques for developing an abundant mindset that will draw prosperity and money into your life.

Your potential can be fully realized and the boundless possibilities of the universe can be accessed by developing an attitude of plenty and worthiness. You will see wealth as something that is available to you right now, rather than something that is kept for other people.

The secret to gaining unbounded wealth and prosperity is changing your perspective.

THE INFLUENCE OF FAITH

For a brief period, picture your mind as a garden, with your thoughts serving as the seeds you plant. Which type of garden are you growing? We'll look at the influence of belief and how your beliefs affect your financial situation. You will create the conditions for riches to come into your life naturally if you cultivate an abundance- and prosperity-oriented attitude and embrace beliefs that support it.

One key idea that greatly influences how our financial reality is shaped is the power of belief. It's the notion that our financial results are directly influenced by the attitudes, ideas, and behaviors we have around money. In essence, our beliefs about money have the capacity to either enable us to attain financial success or prevent us from realizing our greatest potential.

Our attitudes on money are frequently deeply rooted and shaped by a variety of elements, including our experiences, culture, and upbringing. Both conscious and subconscious ideas have a role in determining how we view abundance, prosperity, and money.

A person may acquire a scarcity mindset—the conviction that there is never enough money for everyone—if they were raised in a home where money was always tight and scarcity was the norm. Because they believe they would never be able to achieve financial security or prosperity, they may find it difficult to save, invest, or take financial risks.

However, an abundance mindset—the conviction that there is more than enough income and resources for everyone—may emerge in a person who was nurtured in an atmosphere where possibilities were abundant and money was perceived as ample. With this kind of thinking, people can approach money with assurance, hope, and a readiness to take measured chances in order to achieve their financial objectives.

When we examine the idea of self-fulfilling prophecies, the strength of belief is made very clear. Within the field of psychology, a self-fulfilling prophecy refers to a belief or expectation that shapes behavior in a way that brings about the fulfillment of that belief or expectation. In terms of money, this means that our attitudes toward money have the power to influence our choices and behaviors in ways that eventually serve to validate those attitudes.

For instance, if someone thinks they're not talented or intelligent enough to make a six-figure salary, they can unintentionally hinder their attempts to pursue higher-paying jobs. Because they secretly think they're not deserving of financial success, they could shy away from asking for promotions, hesitate to negotiate better pay, or neglect to invest in their continued education and skill development.

On the other hand, an individual who really believes that they may attain financial prosperity might handle their finances with assurance, tenacity, and fortitude. Knowing that their opinions and behaviors are in line with their success vision, they might set lofty objectives, take calculated chances, and persevere in the face of difficulties.

Essentially, the way we view our financial realities is filtered by our attitudes about money. We are more likely to recognize possibilities, act, and eventually reach our financial objectives if we think that money is reachable and that we have the ability to generate abundance in our lives. However, we will continue to face shortage and difficulty in our financial life if we cling to restrictive beliefs and negative attitudes about money.

Thankfully, believing power is not static nor unchangeable. We may question and reframe our ideas about money by substituting plenty for scarcity, anxiety for confidence, and opportunity for limitation if we approach the task with awareness, purpose, and effort. We can change the way money works in our lives and bring about the abundance and prosperity we want by developing an optimistic and powerful mindset.

ACCEPTING PLENTY

Being abundant is a manner of life, not merely a mentality. Adopting a perspective and way of life that acknowledges and appreciates the innate wealth in our lives is what it means to embrace abundance. It's the conviction that everyone has access to more than enough of anything, including opportunities, fortune, love, and happiness. By embracing abundance, we may become more aware of the boundless opportunities that are all around us and change our perspective from one of scarcity and lack to one of thankfulness and abundance.

Embracing wealth is really a mentality—a grateful, giving, and hopeful outlook. It's about developing an attitude of thankfulness for the things we have and realizing the plenty that, in spite of the state of affairs, already exists in our lives.

Accepting abundance means changing our mindset from one of scarcity—where we believe there is never enough—to one of abundance—where we acknowledge the abundance of resources, opportunities, and possibilities at our disposal. Rather than concentrating on our shortcomings, we embrace what we have and the limitless possibilities for development and growth. Accepting abundance also means living a rich and satisfying life, not just in terms of money or material belongings, but also in terms of relationships, spirituality, and social impact.

Gratitude is a practice that is essential to accepting abundance. Gratitude is the antidote to scarcity because it makes us appreciate and feel pleased with what we have instead of focusing on what we lack. By developing an attitude of thankfulness, we teach our minds to recognize the richness all around us, even in the seemingly insignificant things.

Fostering an attitude of potential and opportunity is a crucial part of living an abundant life. Rather than considering difficulties and barriers as impediments, we see them as chances for development and education. We approach life with an open mind and curiosity, understanding that every event, no matter how good or bad, has the capacity to provide wisdom.

In the end, choosing to live in excess means making the deliberate decision to change our perspective from one of scarcity to one of plenty. It's about realizing that we can shape our own reality and bring our ideal lives to pass. Adopting an abundant mindset opens the door to a life full of happiness, contentment, and wealth by allowing us to access the limitless reservoir of possibilities both inside and outside of ourselves.

DEVELOPING GRATITUDE

Having gratitude is the key to turning the ordinary into the remarkable. You will draw even more opportunities and things to be grateful for if you adopt an attitude of gratitude and appreciate the abundance that is currently in your life. Prepare to witness the expansion of your wealth in front of your eyes as you unleash the amazing power of appreciation. Gratitude cultivation is a powerful practice that can improve our relationships, mental health, and general well-being. It goes beyond simply saying "thank you" and appreciating the good things in our lives. Essentially, practicing thankfulness is deliberately searching for and recognizing the small and large gifts that come into our lives every day and make them more meaningful.

Being able to change our mindset from one of scarcity to one of abundance is one of the most significant effects of practicing thankfulness. By deliberately concentrating on the things for which we are thankful, we can teach our minds to recognize the abundance all around us, even in the face of difficulties or misfortune. Gratitude helps us to see and appreciate the abundance that is already in our lives rather than focusing on what we lack.

The potential of practicing thankfulness to promote joy and happiness is one of its most potent features. Empathy training has been linked to higher levels of happiness, better moods, and higher levels of life satisfaction, according to a number of studies. We establish a positive feedback loop that amplifies our sense of contentment and well-being when we dwell on the positive aspects of our lives and express gratitude for them.

Gratitude has been connected to several physical health advantages in addition to its beneficial effects on our relationships and emotional well-being. According to studies, cultivating thankfulness can enhance immunity, enhance sleep quality, and lessen anxiety and stress symptoms. Our physical health and well-being are enhanced when we practice thankfulness in addition to our minds and emotions.

TAKING INITIATIVE

Wishing for money is one thing, but the real magic comes in doing.. You will discover how to create a potent energy vortex that draws prosperity and abundance into your life by coordinating your ideas, beliefs, and behaviors with your desires. Prepare to take charge of your life and begin realizing your aspirations.

Taking inspired action is following your inner guidance and intuition to go forward with passion and purpose. It entails venturing outside of our comfort zones, accepting uncertainty, and resolutely and bravely pursuing our goals. Fear or responsibility do not motivate inspired behavior; rather, it is a strong sense of alignment with our own objectives and beliefs.

We connect with the flow of plenty and harness the creative power of the cosmos when we act with inspiration. We follow our hearts' guidance and trust our intuition rather than waiting for the ideal opportunity or looking for approval from others. Frequently, this results in unforeseen prospects, coincidences, and discoveries that advance us toward our objectives.

We must adopt a mindset of possibility and opportunity in order to take inspired action, letting go of self-doubt and limiting beliefs. It all comes down to having faith in our own abilities to materialize our dreams and achieving them in spite of any roadblocks or disappointments we may experience.

Being willing to take chances, make errors, and grow from our experiences is, at its core, what it means to take inspired action and pursue our goals. In order to navigate the way ahead, we must embrace the unknown and have faith that the cosmos has our back.

GETTING RID OF LIMITING THOUGHTS

In order to overcome limiting beliefs, we must recognize and confront the unfavorable ideas and presumptions that prevent us from realizing our greatest potential. It takes guts, self-awareness, and a readiness to question the narratives we tell ourselves about our worth and ability. We can free ourselves from the limitations of fear and self-doubt by redefining our beliefs and substituting them with ones that empower us. This will allow us to see new options and chances for development and achievement.

Now that you know how powerful belief is, how to think abundantly, how to be grateful, how important inspired action is, and how to break through limiting ideas, you can start living a life of boundless wealth and happiness. Recall that having riches involves leading a life of richness, contentment, and freedom in all spheres of one's life—not just financial prosperity. Thus, set out to realize your most ambitious goals—the path to financial success begins now!

CHAPTER THREE
CREATING SEVERAL REVENUE SOURCES

It's time to focus on creating several streams of income now that you have a good grasp of your current financial situation and a wealth-oriented mindset. This chapter will discuss the range of revenue-generating options at your disposal and how to use them to reach six-figure success.

The days of obtaining all of your revenue from one source are long gone. To establish stability and security in your finances in the fast-paced, constantly-evolving economy of today, it's critical to diversify your sources of income.

First, we'll talk about the value of diversity and the reasons having several sources of income is so important. The advantages of having a variety of sources of income will be discussed, including improved flexibility, resilience to market fluctuations, and financial security.

We will next get into some useful techniques for creating various revenue streams. This could be launching a side business, doing freelance work, offering advice, or developing digital goods and services. We'll go through the benefits and drawbacks of each strategy as well as how to select the best revenue sources for your needs and goals in light of your abilities and interests.

But generating various revenue streams is about more than just increasing your income; it's also about living a fulfilling and abundant life. You may follow your passions, take advantage of fresh possibilities, and build the life you've always wanted by diversifying your sources of income.

DIVERSIFICATION IS NECESSARY TO LOWER RISK AND RAISE STABILITY

A key idea in the realm of finance is diversification, which is the practice of distributing investments throughout a range of assets in order to reduce risk and increase return. In a similar vein, creating several revenue streams entails diversifying your sources of income, minimizing your reliance on any one source, and boosting the durability and stability of your financial portfolio.

Developing various sources of income helps you construct a safety net against job loss, economic downturns, and unanticipated financial losses. You now have many streams of income that keep you afloat even in the event that one is momentarily interrupted, so you are no longer dependent only on one paycheck to pay your bills.

PASSIVE INCOME POWER: MAKING MONEY WHILE YOU SLEEP

Making money that requires little effort or continuous work on your side is known as passive income, and it is one of the most alluring features of creating several revenue sources. A multitude of sources, such as rental properties, royalties, dividends, interest income, and internet enterprises, can provide passive income streams.

Your time, abilities, and resources can be leveraged to create passive income streams that bring in money even while you're not working. By giving you financial stability, independence, and flexibility, this passive income can let you follow your hobbies, spend time with the people you love, and live your life how you see fit.

Passive income streams provide income even while you're not actively working, as contrast to active income, which demands you to exchange time for money. Here are some instances of passive income along with information on how to get them:

1. Rental Properties: One of the most well-liked strategies for making passive income is real estate investing. Buying rental properties allows you to possibly profit from property appreciation over time in addition to receiving monthly rental revenue from renters. Start by learning about real estate markets, examining possible properties, and taking into account variables like cash flow forecasts, location, and rental demand.

Dividend stocks: By purchasing companies that pay dividends, you can systematically increase your income through dividend payments, which are usually made either quarterly or annually. Shares of businesses that pay out a portion of their income as dividends to shareholders are known as dividend stocks. In order to assemble a portfolio of dividend stocks, look at businesses that have a track record of reliable dividend payments, solid financials, and room to develop.

3. Royalties: Money obtained in exchange for the use of creative works, patents, trademarks, or copyrights is known as a royalty. For instance, artists receive royalties from streaming and licensing music, authors from book sales, and innovators from product sales. To get paid royalties, either produce valuable intellectual property or use royalty trusts or licensing agreements to invest in already-existing intellectual property.

4. Digital items: Another method to make passive income is to create and market digital items like software, e-books, online courses, and digital downloads. A digital product you've made can be sold to customers again and again without having to pay for further manufacturing or delivery expenses. In order to produce digital goods, choose a specialized market, provide insightful material or solutions, and advertise your goods via online stores or sales channels.

Affiliate marketing entails endorsing goods or services from other businesses and obtaining a commission for every purchase or recommendation made via your affiliate link. Via email newsletters, blogs, social media platforms, websites, and other marketing methods, you can advertise affiliate goods. In order to be successful with affiliate marketing, pick goods or services that complement you consider the needs and interests of your audience, offer insightful advice and material, and monitor the effectiveness of your affiliate connections.

6. Peer-to-peer Lending: Peer-to-peer lending networks enable people to lend money to others in return for interest payments by bringing borrowers and investors together. You can profit passively from your investments by investing in

peer-to-peer loans and collecting interest. In order to reduce risk, spread your investments over a number of loans, evaluate the creditworthiness and risk profiles of borrowers, and investigate peer-to-peer lending platforms before making any commitments.

Depending on your abilities, preferences, and financial situation, there are a plethora of additional options for passive income streams; these are just a few examples. Passive income, which might come from investments in stocks, real estate, digital goods, or intellectual property, can be a great way to achieve financial independence, stability, and wealth building.

DEVELOPING FINANCIAL INDEPENDENCE AND RESILIENCE

You can improve your financial security and stability as well as your ability to withstand market and economic volatility by diversifying your sources of income. You get more control over your financial future and become less susceptible to the whims of a particular employer, industry, or economic sector.
Furthermore, creating several sources of income is essential to reaching financial independence, which is the situation in which you can live life as you choose without being dependent on a regular work or paycheck when your passive income surpasses your expenses.

Establishing financial independence and resilience together lay the groundwork for a safe and prosperous future. While financial independence enables us to prosper independent of external circumstances, resilience enables us to weather life's unavoidable storms. Let's examine the intersection of these two ideas using some interesting and memorable examples:

1. Weathering Financial Storms: Picture yourself in the event of an abrupt layoff or unanticipated medical bill. Having a financial safety net to fall back on in trying times is a key component of building resilience. This might be an emergency fund, which serves as a safety net for your finances so you can pay for necessities without using credit cards or loans. An emergency fund covers you from life's financial downpours, much like a good umbrella does against the rain.

2. Diversifying Your Income Streams: Building a house on shaky footing is riskier and less stable than relying only on one source of income. To achieve financial independence, you must diversify your sources of income in order to generate numerous revenue streams. Consider yourself a freelance graphic designer who also makes passive money from the internet sales of digital art. You can build a safety net to shield yourself from the ups and downs of the freelance market by diversifying your sources of income.

3. Investing in Yourself: To prosper monetarily, you must invest in yourself, just like a plant needs water and sunlight to develop. This could entail seeking opportunities for personal growth, learning new talents, or advancing your education. As an illustration, let's say you work in marketing and decide to take a course on digital marketing tactics. Investing in skill development can boost your earning

potential and fortify you against competitors in the labor market.

4. Developing a Growth Mindset: Being resilient means accepting change and adjusting to novel situations, in addition to persevering through setbacks. Similar to this, acquiring financial independence necessitates developing a growth mentality in which obstacles are viewed as chances for development. Think of yourself as a bamboo plant that, when faced with hardship, bends but does not breaks. Your ability to adapt and embrace change will put you in a position to succeed financially in the long run.

5. Developing Mindfulness and Gratitude: Having an abundant and resilient attitude is facilitated by practicing gratitude, which also cultivates a sense of abundance. Whether it's a steaming cup of coffee or a supportive comment from a friend, pause to acknowledge and be grateful for the little victories and gifts in your life. You can develop resilience from the inside out by practicing mindfulness and appreciation, which will help you overcome obstacles and remain committed to your financial objectives.

To put it briefly, developing financial independence and resilience is similar to building a strong bridge that will carry you through life's choppy moments. You build the foundation for a stable, secure, and prosperous future by having a growth mindset, investing in yourself, diversifying your sources of income, and practicing thankfulness.

TAKING CHARGE OF YOUR OWN SUCCESS

By taking charge of your life, utilizing your inner qualities, and generating chances for development and accomplishment, you may empower yourself for success. It entails developing a resilient, self-assured, and confident mindset based on the knowledge that you are in control of your own fate. To realize your greatest potential, you must feed your mind, body, and soul, just like a seed needs water and sunlight to grow into a powerful tree. This could entail establishing challenging objectives, persevering through setbacks, and looking for resources and assistance to assist you along the path. By giving authority by positioning yourself for success, you open up a world of limitless opportunities and build a fulfilling, passionate, and purposeful life for yourself.

In summary, developing several revenue streams is an attitude—a philosophy of opportunity, abundance, and empowerment—rather than just a financial tactic. You build a strong foundation for prosperity, security, and financial freedom by diversifying your sources of income.

Therefore, keep in mind that you have the ability to accumulate wealth, regardless of where you are in your journey to financial independence or how you want to increase the sources of income you currently have. You may open the door to an infinitely potential world and build an abundant and prosperous life for yourself and your loved ones if you have the imagination, perseverance, and courage to take calculated risks

CHAPTER FOUR

EXAMINING VARIOUS REVENUE SOURCES: CHARTING THE COURSE FOR ECONOMIC INDEPENDENCE

In today's expansive world of limitless possibilities and abundance, achieving financial freedom has become an adventure in self-discovery that takes people down a variety of paths, each with its own special potential for wealth and prosperity. A wide range of income choices exist, ranging from conventional work to self-employment, passive income sources to alternative investments. This diversity and complexity of options encourages investigation and learning. We set out on a quest to learn about the various sources of income that are open to people who want to accumulate wealth, establish financial stability, and realize their aspirations.

THE CHANGING FACE OF EMPLOYMENT: TRANSITIONING TO ENTREPRENEURSHIP

The old work model of decades ago was centered on the idea of secure employment, which is defined as a full-time job with benefits, a predictable salary, and a clear career path. But just as the world economy has changed, so has the nature of work, with more people seeing gig economy, freelancing, and entrepreneurship as respectable substitutes for traditional employment.

Through entrepreneurship, people may design their own lives, follow their hobbies, start enterprises, and make money whenever and however they see fit. Entrepreneurship offers a route to financial independence and self-sufficiency, enabling people to utilize their abilities, interests, and skills to add value and make money, whether it's through founding an online business, freelancing as a consultant, or launching a startup.

Now let's consider Alex.;
There once was a young man named Alex who lived in the bustling metropolis of Oakville. Alex had always had a burning desire to be financially independent; it was like a beacon shining brilliantly inside of him. Alex set out to investigate the wide range of income streams that would help him reach his ultimate objective because he was driven by a desire for success and a desire for adventure.

He stumbled into a thriving artisan market in the center of the city, where his adventure started. Alex felt a spark of excitement kindle within him, inspired by the sellers' innovation and passion. Choosing to give woodworking a go, he produced exquisite hand-carved statues and elaborate furniture that captivated the attention of onlookers.

With the success of his woodworking business, Alex came to the realization that there were a plethora of additional prospects just waiting to be explored. Entering the realm of digital entrepreneurship, he opened an online store to present his works to a worldwide customer base. Alex felt proud and accomplished with every transaction, knowing that he was getting closer to realizing his goals.

Alex, though, was not one to sit back and take it all in. He decided to investigate the world of passive income since he understood that diversity was necessary for true financial freedom. He became fascinated with investing and spent a lot of time reading books and using the internet to research real estate and the stock market.

With his newfound knowledge and tenacity, Alex started assembling a portfolio of dividend-paying stocks and real estate, generating many sources of consistent passive income that deposited into his bank account. He felt liberated and empowered with every investment, knowing that he was taking charge of his financial future.

Thanks to his relentless drive for success and his entrepreneurial mentality, Alex's empire grew throughout the years. He encouraged others to follow in his footsteps as he grew his woodworking company and increasingly diversified his investments.

The next time you dream of being financially independent, keep Alex's story in mind. Whether you're investing in the stock market or creating woodworking masterpieces, there are a plethora of chances just waiting to be discovered. You too may set your own path to financial freedom and a better future if you have the guts, the will, and the desire to take chances.

USING PASSIVE INCOME TO YOUR ADVANTAGE

Investigating varied income options can also be done through passive income, which is a form of income that needs little continuing work or active participation. In contrast to regular job or active business endeavors, passive income streams give you a sense of financial security and freedom because they keep making money even when you're not actively working.

Dividend-paying stocks, rental properties, and royalties from creative works are just a few of the many methods to get passive income. One way that investing in real estate can yield income is through rental properties; similarly, investing in dividends can provide investors with consistent income through dividend payments made by publicly traded firms.

THE EMERGENCE OF THE DIGITAL ECONOMY: PROSPECTS IN THE VIRTUAL WORLD

The growth of the digital economy in recent years has provided a multitude of options for people looking for other sources of income. The internet has revolutionized the way we work, communicate, and do business. It has opened up new channels for making money and connecting with clients globally, from e-commerce to digital marketing to online education.

E-commerce sites such as Amazon, Shopify, and Etsy give people the chance to sell goods online to millions of customers worldwide; digital marketing gives people the chance to monetize content and reach audiences through sponsored content, affiliate marketing, and advertising revenue; and online education sites such as Udemy and Coursera let people make and sell online courses to students all over the world.

NON-TRADITIONAL INCOME OPPORTUNITIES: EXAMINING ALTERNATIVE INVESTMENTS

Apart from conventional work, self-employment, passive earnings, and internet-based prospects, an array of alternative investments provide distinctive avenues for generating revenue. Alternative investments give people the chance to diversify their portfolios and possibly generate significant returns. Examples of these investments include peer-to-peer lending, cryptocurrencies, art, and collectibles.

Through peer-to-peer lending systems, people can lend money to others and earn interest. These platforms connect borrowers and investors. Although still in its infancy and very volatile, cryptocurrency presents a huge profit opportunity for risk-tolerant investors. On the other hand, investments in art and collectibles give people the chance to make tangible goods that might increase in value over time.

RISK AND RETURN BALANCING: THE SIGNIFICANCE OF DIVERSIFICATION

Even while looking into a variety of income streams might lead to financial success and independence, it's crucial to understand that investing entails risk. Many factors can affect the performance of income-generating projects, including market instability, economic downturns, and unforeseen catastrophes.

Because of this, variety is essential. You can lower risk and raise the possibility that you will meet your financial objectives by distributing your investments among a range of traditional and alternative income streams. By utilizing various sources of income and investment vehicles, diversification offers stability and resilience when faced with unforeseen circumstances.

To sum up, investigating a variety of income streams is about building a life of plenty, independence, and contentment rather than only making money. It's important to identify the correct combination of income streams that fit your objectives, values, and aspirations, whether that means looking for traditional work, starting your own business, passive income, online opportunities, or alternative investments.

So embrace the spirit of discovery as you set out on your path to financial freedom. Aspire to continuous learning and development throughout your life, be open to new chances, and be prepared to take measured risks. You may forge your way to financial independence and build a prosperous life for yourself and your loved ones if you have tenacity, determination, and the flexibility to change.

CHAPTER FIVE
TECHNIQUES FOR INCREASING YOUR INCOME

The secret to obtaining financial independence and abundance is scaling your revenue. You can quicken the process of generating wealth and reaching your financial objectives by utilizing streams and strategic growth tactics

GAIN MARKETABLE TALENTS:

Make an investment to learn talents that employers are looking for. This might be accomplished by online learning, career training, or traditional schooling.
--Determine In-Demand Skills: Examine employment markets and sectors to determine which skills are in high demand. Technical abilities like coding, digital marketing, and data analysis as well as soft talents like problem-solving, communication, and leadership may fall under this category.
--Invest in Education and Training: To develop new skills or improve current ones, sign up for classes, workshops, or certification programs. This could be accomplished through specialist training facilities, internet resources, or conventional educational establishments.
--Seek Practical Experience: In order to get real-world experience in your desired industry, consider volunteering, interning, or doing freelance work. Practical experience shows prospective employers or clients your abilities and aids in the application of academic information.

--Engage in Continuous Learning: Read books, subscribe to industry blogs, watch webinars, or join online forums to stay current on trends and advancements in the field. Maintaining your edge over the competition and keeping your abilities current requires constant learning.

--Create a Portfolio: Use projects, case studies, or creative work to highlight your abilities and achievements. In addition to showcasing your experience, a solid portfolio is a valuable tool for drawing in new customers or employers.

Network and Seek Mentorship: Utilize industry associations, LinkedIn, and networking events to make connections with professionals in your sector. Seeking mentoring from seasoned professionals can offer insightful advice and helpful direction as you advance your career and skill set.

You may raise your value on the job market and create new avenues for income growth and professional advancement by actively cultivating marketable abilities.

NEGOTIATE YOUR SALARY:

When starting a new job or during performance reviews, don't be hesitant to bargain for your pay. To support your request for a raise, look at industry norms and emphasize your value.

The ability to successfully negotiate your pay is essential and can have a big impact on your financial situation. Following are some essential guidelines for successful wage negotiations:

--Study Market Standards: Learn about industry norms and typical compensation for your role before engaging in any talks. You will have significant negotiating power if you are aware of the going rate.

---In order to show the firm how valuable you are, it is important that you succinctly state your successes, experiences, and talents. You can improve your negotiating position by emphasizing your contributions and how they support the objectives of the company.

---Establish Reasonable Expectations: Calculate your ideal pay by taking into account your experience, education, and local cost of living. As important as setting lofty goals is, you also need to be grounded in reality and mindful of the financial limitations of your organization.

---Practice being assertive: Negotiations should be approached with professionalism, respect, and a strong, confident demeanor. Make sure you make your compensation expectations clear, and be ready to stand up for yourself if needed.

---Take Total Compensation into Account: Base pay is only one aspect of salary discussions. Other considerations include incentives like stock options, bonuses, benefits, and room for professional advancement. You may make more educated selections by analyzing the entire compensation package. Have a target wage in mind, but also be open to negotiating and making concessions when needed. Flexibility and openness to compromise are key. In order to increase the offer's total worth, take into account extra benefits or different payment options.

----Decide on the Best Time: When negotiating a pay, timing is everything. Best to wait until you receive an offer of employment or until you can prove your worth to the organization in performance assessments. In the interview process, try not to bring up salary too soon.

---During discussions, engage in Active Listening by paying close attention to the employer's queries and concerns. Developing a rapport with them and answering any questions or concerns they may have might help to promote fruitful dialogues.

You may argue for just remuneration and put yourself in a position to succeed financially in your profession over the long run by becoming an expert in salary negotiation.

LAUNCH A SIDE BUSINESS:

To launch a side business, explore your interests and abilities. This could include working as a freelancer, giving advice, running an internet store, or providing services like graphic design or tuition.
Creating a side business can be a fulfilling way to follow your interests and boost your income. Here are some essential guidelines for launching a side business successfully:

1. Determine Your Interest or Ability: Select a company idea that plays to your abilities, experience, and areas of interest. Whether your interest is photography, graphic design, coaching, or crafting, choosing a niche will boost your enthusiasm and drive.

2. Study the Market: Find out who your target market is, how much demand there is for your goods or services, and what your competitors are up to. To position your organization for success, analyze market trends, consumer preferences, and prospective pricing plans.

3.Create a company Plan: Compile your goals, target market, pricing strategy, marketing approaches, and financial projections into a succinct and understandable company plan. A clear strategy will act as your company's road map and keep you concentrated on your objectives.

4.Set Aside Time and Resources: Assess the amount of time and resources you can commit to your side venture while maintaining your regular employment and personal obligations. To guarantee the viability of your endeavor, set a reasonable timeline and make prudent resource allocations.

5.Develop Your Brand: To set your company apart from the competition and establish a solid reputation in the marketplace, make branding investments. Create an iconic brand name, logo, and other visual elements that speak to your target market and represent the values of your company.

6.Establish Your Business: Establish a specific workplace or online platform for doing business operations, register your company, and acquire any licenses or permits that are required. To optimize your company's operations, create effective procedures for handling orders, enquiries, and client relations.

7.Promote Your Business: To draw clients and raise awareness of your side gig, create a thorough marketing plan. Reach your target demographic more successfully by combining offline and online marketing strategies including social media marketing, content production, email campaigns, networking events, and collaborations.

8. Assure Exceptional Customer Service: Put the needs of your clients first by offering top-notch goods and services together with outstanding customer support. As you continue to develop your offerings and improve the customer experience, cultivate a solid rapport with your clients and welcome their comments.

9. Keep Track of Your Development: Continually assess your company's performance in relation to your targets. Monitor important indicators like sales, revenue, costs, and client feedback to gauge your success and make well-informed choices that can enhance your company's operations.

You can open up new avenues for revenue production and personal fulfillment by paying attention to these essential elements and beginning and growing your side business with initiative. You can make your passion a successful business and reach greater success and financial freedom with commitment, persistence, and ingenuity.

INVEST WISELY:

You may make your money work for you by allocating it to passive income-producing assets like dividend-paying funds, equities, and real estate.
To accumulate money and reach financial objectives, prudent investment is required. The following are important ideas for prudent investing:

---Establish Specific Financial Objectives: Identify your goals with money: are you saving for retirement, buying a house, or paying for your kids' schooling? Your investing plan and risk tolerance can be ascertained with the aid of well-defined goals.

2. Educate Yourself: Make the effort to become knowledgeable about various investing possibilities, including retirement accounts, stocks, bonds, and mutual funds, as well as real estate. To make wise judgments, be aware of the dangers and possible rewards connected to each investment.

To minimize risk and optimize returns, it is advisable to diversify your investments across multiple industries and asset classes. By reducing the impact of individual investment losses, diversification helps insulate your portfolio from market swings.

4. Invest for the Long Term: Take a long-term view of the market and refrain from acting rashly in response to transient swings. Refrain from trying to time the market or follow fads in investments and instead stay focused on your financial objectives.

5. Get Started Earlier and Continually: By starting your investments early and making consistent contributions to your investment accounts, you can benefit from the compounding effect. Compound interest can cause even modest, regular donations to increase dramatically over time.

6. Minimize Costs: Over time, investing fees, commissions, and taxes can reduce your profits. To increase your after-tax profits, choose for low-cost investment options like index funds or exchange-traded funds (ETFs) and take into account tax-efficient investing techniques.

7. Remain Educated and Flexible: Update yourself on market and economic trends that could affect your assets. Regularly review your portfolio and be ready to modify your investment plan in response to changes in the market or in your financial circumstances.

8. Seek specialist Advice: To assist you in creating a customized investment plan that is suited to your objectives, risk tolerance, and time horizon, think about collaborating with a licensed financial advisor or investing specialist. You can get invaluable advice and knowledge from a financial advisor to help you deal with the challenges of investing.

You may attain your long-term financial goals and provide a strong foundation for financial stability by paying attention to these important points and making prudent investments. Recall that success in investing is a journey.

CREATE SEVERAL REVENUE STREAMS

To lessen dependency on a single source, diversify your revenue streams. This could involve earning money through affiliate marketing, royalties, dividends, rental income, or the creation of digital goods. This has been covered in more detail in earlier chapters.

SIMPLIFY YOUR SOURCES OF INCOME

To grow your income without adding to your workload, automation is essential. Seek methods for automating your sources of passive income so that you can leave them running with no daily effort or involvement. Take into account using robo-advisors to handle your investment portfolio, employing property managers to supervise your rental properties, or setting up procedures and software to simplify the running of your internet business. You may focus on growing your business and exploring new prospects by freeing up time by automating repetitive operations and procedures.

BOOST YOUR INFLUENCE

To scale your profits and maximize your income potential, you must reach a wider audience. Seek to expand your audience or clientele for your passive revenue sources. For instance, you could want to think about diversifying your real estate holdings by adding properties in other regions or growing your online business to other markets. You can access new revenue streams and seize fresh chances for development and advancement by broadening your horizons.

ENHANCE YOUR CREDENTIALS

To raise your earning potential, keep investing in your professional and educational growth. Think about obtaining specialized training, certificates, or advanced degrees. Investing in additional coursework, certifications, or skill development courses pertinent to your industry is necessary to upgrade your credentials. It's about improving your knowledge, remaining up to date with industry trends, and being more marketable. Upgrading credentials can help people get better jobs, demand more money, and adjust to the changing needs of the labor market.

NEVER STOP LEARNING AND DEVELOPING

Maintaining your competitive edge and increasing your income in the quickly evolving modern economy requires ongoing education and personal development. Invest in your own development by learning new things that will improve your capacity to create wealth and earn passive income. Participate in conferences, seminars, and workshops; take online courses; and consult mentors and subject-matter experts for advice. You can take advantage of opportunities, adjust to new obstacles, and increase your earning potential by always learning and developing.

INVEST YOUR PROFITS BACK

Another effective tactic for growing your earnings is to reinvest your profits. Reinvest your passive income back into your income-generating assets rather than just spending or saving it to increase your returns over time. By reinvesting your earnings, you can attain exponential growth and quicken the process of accumulating wealth. Compounding can greatly boost your long-term wealth, regardless of whether you're reinvesting stock dividends, real estate rental revenue, or earnings from your web business.

USE OF LEVERAGE
Using financial leverage to scale your earnings and increase your return on investment is a smart move. Seek ways to use leverage to raise your exposure to assets that generate income and to buy more with your money. Take into account employing leverage, for instance, while financing the acquisition of rental properties, making margin investments

in dividend-paying stocks, or growing your web company through debt financing. But, before taking on more debt, it's crucial to use leverage sensibly and thoroughly weigh the hazards.

CREATE CONNECTIONS AND NETWORK

Creating connections through networking can lead to new business prospects and job chances. To grow your network, go to industry events, join associations for professionals, and make use of social media.
To increase your income and open up new growth prospects, networking and teamwork are crucial. Become connected with like-minded people, business owners, and financiers who may provide encouragement, direction, and joint venture opportunities. To grow your network and make connections with possible partners and collaborators, join networking groups, go to industry events, and engage in online communities. You can increase your profits and reach your financial objectives by cooperating and networking with others to take advantage of their knowledge, assets, and connections.

To increase your income, keep in mind that you must be committed, persistent, and willing to push yourself beyond your comfort zone. You can work toward reaching your financial objectives and gradually raise your income by putting these strategies into practice and being proactive in your search of financial progress.

CHAPTER SIX

EFFECTIVE BUDGETING AND SAVINGS STRATEGIES: ESTABLISHING A STRONG FINANCIAL BASE

The two main foundations of successful money management are saving and budgeting. Strategic budgeting and saving can help you take charge of your money, reach your financial objectives, and lay the groundwork for long-term stability and prosperity. We'll go over some practical budgeting and saving techniques in this tutorial to help you handle your money sensibly and reach financial independence.

MAKE DEFINITE FINANCIAL GOALS

Establishing specific financial goals is the first stage in a smart budget and saving process. Establish your financial goals, whether they be reaching a certain financial milestone, paying off debt, preparing for retirement, or accumulating an emergency fund. When creating goals, make sure they are precise, quantifiable, and doable. You should also specify deadlines for each goal. Having specific financial goals can help you keep motivated and focused on your goals by giving you a road map for your budgeting and saving efforts.

MAKE A FINANCIAL PLAN

Make a budget to aid in your efficient money management after you've determined your financial objectives. An extensive plan that describes your earnings, outlays, and savings objectives for a given time frame—say, a month or a year—is called a budget. After you've listed all of your sources of income—including bonuses, salaries, and investment returns—deduct your fixed costs, which include loan payments, rent, and utilities. A percentage of your income should go toward savings and discretionary costs like eating out and entertainment. Keep track of your spending to make sure you're remaining within your budget.

PRIORITIZE YOUR OWN NEEDS.

Paying yourself first is one of the best ways to save money. This entails setting aside some of your money for savings before you cover your bills or other non-essential spending. To make sure you're continuously saving money, set up automatic transfers from your checking account to your retirement account or savings account each month. Saving money will become second nature to you if you prioritize it and handle it like any other fixed expense. This will help you reach your financial objectives without your having to think about it.

APPLY 50/30/20 RULE

A straightforward guideline for creating a successful budget is the 50/30/20 rule. This rule states that 50% of your income should go into necessities like housing, utilities, and groceries; 30% should go toward wants like dining out and entertainment; and 20% should go toward debt reduction and savings. Aim to save at least 20% of your monthly salary to create an emergency fund, save for retirement, and accomplish other long-term goals. You can adjust these percentages according to your unique situation and financial goals.

MONITOR YOUR EXPENSES

Regularly check your spending to keep an eye on your spending and find places where you may save money. Whether you do it by hand or with budgeting applications or software, keep a thorough record of your spending and divide it up into fixed, variable, and discretionary costs. Examine your spending habits on a regular basis to locate areas where you may make savings or find ways to negotiate lower costs, shop around for better offers, or cut out unneeded purchases completely.

ADOPT A FRUGAL MINDSET

Being thrifty doesn't mean denying yourself the things you love; rather, it involves being aware of your expenditures and figuring out how to live within your means. By using coupons, browsing sales, and finding free or inexpensive activities, you can find ways to reduce the cost of regular costs like groceries, transportation, and entertainment. Prioritize spending on items that make you happy and fulfilled while reducing wasteful spending by practicing mindful spending, which involves differentiating necessities from wants.

CREATE AN EMERGENCY FUND.

Cultivating an emergency reserve to offset unforeseen costs and financial hardships is a critical component of smart saving. Save enough money in a money market fund or conveniently accessible savings account to cover three to six months' worth of living costs at least. Your financial security and peace of mind will come from knowing that you have an emergency fund in place to handle any unanticipated events.

REGULARLY REVIEW AND MAKE ADJUSTMENTS TO YOUR BUDGET

Last but not least, periodically review and modify your budget to account for variations in your earnings, outlays, and financial objectives. Since life is dynamic, your budget should be adaptable enough to take into account changes in your financial circumstances. Make any necessary adjustments to your budget to bring your spending in line with your priorities and values. Regularly evaluate your budget to make sure you're on track to reach your goals.

Building a strong financial foundation and attaining financial success need the ability to budget and save strategically. You can take charge of your money, lessen financial stress, and reach your long-term financial goals by setting clear financial goals, making a budget, paying yourself first, adhering to the 50/30/20 rule, tracking your expenditures, practicing frugality, setting up an emergency fund, and routinely reviewing and adjusting your budget. You may accumulate riches, become financially independent, and design the life you've always wanted with perseverance, dedication, and hard work.

CHAPTER SEVEN

THE BUDGETING BLUEPRINT: A PATHWAY TO ECONOMIC INDEPENDENCE

A young woman named GRACE used to reside in the thriving metropolis of Prosperity Falls. Like many people in her town, GRACE was ambitious, industrious, and ready to create a better future for her family and herself. But even with her best efforts, she could never seem to make ends meet and was always stressed out about money and overwhelmed by debt and obligations.

GRACE was determined to improve her financial circumstances, so she set out to learn the techniques of efficient budgeting, which would allow her to take charge of her money and realize her aspirations of being financially independent. She had no idea that her path would enable her to live an abundant life and change her perspective on money.

The Wake-Up

GRACE's journey started when she had an epiphany, realizing that her existing spending patterns were not beneficial to her. She was startled to learn how much money she was wasting on pointless costs like eating out, shopping, and entertainment when she sat down one evening to go over her bank accounts and bills. She came to the realization that controlling her spending and putting in place a budgeting plan would enable her to handle her finances more skillfully, both of which were necessary if she was to meet her financial objectives.

GRACE decided to learn about the fundamentals of wise budgeting because she was ready to make a change. She went through books, articles, and internet resources like wild, consulting professionals for advice and learning about various approaches and tactics for creating a budget. Eager to discover the most effective method for her, she experimented with a number of budgeting techniques, including the envelope system, zero-based budgeting, and the 50/30/20 rule.

Budgetary Plan

Equipped with erudition and resoluteness, GRACE set out to create her own customized financial plan, or budgeting blueprint, which would enable her to fulfill her financial objectives and regain control over her resources. With a budgeting system that reflected her values and priorities, she was able to live within her means and still enjoy the little things in life. She was inspired by the ideas of simplicity, mindfulness, and flexibility.

Tracking her expenditures and classifying her expenses formed the foundation of GRACE's budgeting plan. She spent money on housing, transportation, groceries, entertainment, and other areas, and she made a comprehensive spreadsheet to track her earnings and outlays. Keeping a close eye on her expenditures allowed her to see areas where she might make savings and improve understanding of her financial patterns.

The Significance of Setting Priorities

GRACE came to understand the value of prioritization as she continued her budgeting adventure. This involved determining what her requirements and wants were and spending her resources accordingly. She set priorities for her short- and long-term financial goals according to their urgency and significance. She deliberately tried to direct her finances toward the things that were most important to her, whether it was saving for a dream vacation, paying off debt, or creating an emergency fund.

She implemented the 50/30/20 rule, a straightforward budgeting principle, to help her distribute her income wisely and prioritize her spending. Fifty percent of her salary was allocated to necessities like housing and utilities, thirty percent to wants like leisure and eating out, and twenty percent to savings and debt reduction. Following this guideline allowed GRACE to balance taking care of her current needs with making plans for the future.

The Travels Commence

Equipped with her budgeting guide, GRACE set off on her path to financial independence with a fresh sense of resolve and self-assurance. She adopted the values of self-control, perseverance, and discipline and made little yet significant adjustments to her spending patterns and way of life. She hunted for sales and discounts, made meals at home rather than going out to dine, and came up with inventive methods to savor life's little joys without going over budget.

GRACE started to observe observable effects as she adhered to her budget. She began to feel less stressed about money, her savings increased, and her debt started to decline. No longer was she overwhelmed by debt and uncertainty; instead, she felt empowered and in charge of her finances. GRACE knew she was making progress toward a better future as each day went by and she got closer to her objective of achieving financial freedom.

The Path Ahead

GRACE faced difficulties and roadblocks as she proceeded on her journey. There were unforeseen costs, unanticipated obstacles, and times of uncertainty and annoyance. Nevertheless, GRACE never wavered in her will to reach her financial objectives, finding courage in the accomplishments she had previously achieved and the future she was striving for.

GRACE became more resilient and stronger after overcoming each obstacle. She gained insightful knowledge about resiliency, tenacity, and the significance of maintaining her focus on her objectives in the face of difficulty. As she proceeded with her journey, she motivated others by sharing her tale of metamorphosis and demonstrating that everything is achievable with perseverance and self-control.

To sum up

An excellent budget is essential to taking charge of your finances and realizing your goals, as demonstrated by GRACE's path to financial independence. You can take charge of your finances and create a better future for yourself and your loved ones by creating a specific budgeting plan, keeping track of your expenditures, setting priorities for your goals, and maintaining focus on your vision. You can live a life of prosperity and fulfillment and attain financial freedom with self-control, perseverance, and dedication to your objectives.

CHAPTER EIGHT

TAKING ADVANTAGE OF AUTOMATED SAVINGS: A ROUTE TO MONETARY INDEPENDENCE

Imagine without having to lift a finger and knowing that you're one step closer to reaching your financial objectives every morning. And therein is the power of automated savings—a straightforward yet remarkably successful plan for accumulating wealth, reaching financial independence, and designing the life you've always wanted. We'll look at how to use automated savings in this guide to manage your money and open the door to a better future.

The Automatic Savings Promise

Many people find that conserving money is a difficult task. Due to the hectic nature of life, it can be simple to overlook saving money for the future when there are bills to pay, costs to meet, and temptations to give in. This is the use of automated savings. You may easily and mentally accumulate money by setting up automatic transfers from your checking account to your investing or savings accounts.

It's now simpler than ever to reach your financial objectives thanks to automated savings, which eliminate the uncertainty and work involved in saving money. You can set it and forget it with automated savings, knowing that your money is working for you in the background, whether you're saving for retirement, a dream vacation, or a rainy day fund.

Automated Savings Mechanisms

Automatic savings are easy to set up and operate. Establish your savings goals first, including the amount and frequency of your savings. Create regular, weekly, biweekly, or monthly automated transfers from your checking account to your investment or savings accounts after that.
Various methods exist for automating savings, based on your financial objectives and personal preferences. Automated transfer services are provided by numerous banks and financial institutions, enabling you to plan regular transfers from your checking account to your savings account. You may also set up automatic savings targets and monitor your success over time with the help of financial management tools or budgeting applications.

Automated Savings' Advantages

Anyone wishing to accumulate wealth and attain financial freedom would find automated savings to be an appealing alternative due to its many advantages:

1.Consistency: Automatic savings make sure that you always save money for the future, no matter how preoccupied or preoccupied you are.

2.Restraint: You can avoid impulsive purchases and unnecessary costs by automating your savings, which will keep you focused and disciplined on your financial objectives.

3.Efficiency: By doing away with the necessity of manually transferring funds to your savings account each month, automated savings save you time and strain. By setting up automatic transfers, you may free up time for other priorities by having your money placed into your savings account on a regular basis.

4.Financial stress can be minimized and peace of mind can be experienced when you actively save money for the future. You may achieve your goals and objectives with the assurance that you're laying a solid financial foundation for your family and yourself when you set up automated savings.

Getting Past Typical Obstacles

Although automated savings have numerous advantages, there are drawbacks as well. Common difficulties consist of:

1.Interruption Fees: If your checking account isn't sufficiently funded to cover automated transfers to your savings account, be wary of overdraft fees. Establish reminders or notifications to keep an eye on your account balance and prevent overdrafts.

2. Updating Your Budget: You might need to make adjustments to your savings targets and budget if your financial circumstances change. React to changes in your income, expenses, and financial objectives by being adaptable and ready to make adjustments to your automated savings strategy.

3 Steer clear of temptation When you have easy access to

money, it can be tempting to take it out of your savings account to cover non-essential costs. Unless there is a genuine emergency or an anticipated need, resist the temptation to take money out of your savings account.

4.Remaining Motivated: Over an extended period of time, it can be difficult to stay motivated and disciplined. To stay inspired and committed to your savings journey, remind yourself of your financial objectives and the advantages of automated savings, such as freedom, peace of mind, and financial stability.

An effective strategy for accumulating wealth, gaining financial independence, and designing the life you want is to set up automatic savings. Taking control of your finances and conserving money can be simple when you use automation to set up regular transfers from your checking account to investment or savings accounts. Automatic savings offer a straightforward and efficient approach to reach your financial objectives and open the door to a better future for you and your loved ones, regardless of whether you're saving for long-term objectives like retirement or short-term goals like a trip.

CHAPTER NINE
JUDICIOUS INVESTING FOR SUSTAINABLE GROWTH

To accumulate wealth, become financially independent, and secure your future, you must make prudent investments for long-term growth. The following are the main things to think about while making long-term investments:

SPECIFY YOUR OBJECTIVES

Establishing your financial goals and objectives is essential before you begin investing. Having well-defined goals will help direct your investment plan, whether your goals include buying a home, supporting your children's school, saving for retirement, or accomplishing other long-term objectives.

RISK ABSORBTION

To choose the right asset allocation for your investing portfolio, evaluate your risk tolerance and time horizon. While older investors may want a more conservative approach with a bigger allocation to bonds or cash, younger investors typically have a longer time horizon and can afford to take on more risk and invest in higher-growth assets like equities.

CHANGE IN STYLE

To spread risk and lessen the effects of market volatility, diversify your investing portfolio throughout several asset classes, industries, and geographical areas. Diversification lowers the chance of suffering substantial losses during market downturns and helps even out investment results over time.

AUTOMOBILES FOR INVESTMENT

Take into account different investment vehicles and instruments that correspond with your investment objectives and risk capacity. For long-term growth, common investing alternatives include equities, bonds, mutual funds, exchange-traded funds (ETFs), real estate, and retirement accounts like IRAs and 401(k)s.

INVESTING IN THE STOCK MARKET

Stock market investments have the potential to increase wealth and provide long-term financial appreciation. Prioritize your investments in reputable businesses with solid growth prospects, competitive advantages, and good fundamentals. When investing in the stock market, have a disciplined mindset rather than attempting to time the market or chase after quick profits.

AVERAGING DOLLAR-COST

Regardless of market conditions, systematically put a fixed amount of money into the market at prearranged intervals. This is known as a dollar-cost averaging technique. By purchasing additional shares at a discount during market downturns, dollar-cost averaging can help mitigate the effects of market volatility.

DIVIDENDS REINVEST

Invest your capital gains and dividends to increase the value of your investments over time. Reinvesting dividends allows you to leverage the long-term wealth-generating power of compounding to build your investment portfolio more quickly.

Keep yourself updated about economic and market developments, but refrain from acting rashly in response to transient shifts in the market. Avoid making rash decisions based on your emotions and instead concentrate on the long-term profitability of your investments.

EVALUATE AND REBALANCE

To keep your target asset allocation, periodically evaluate your investment portfolio and make adjustments as necessary. In order to keep your portfolio in line with your intended allocation and continue working toward your long-term investing objectives, rebalancing entails either purchasing or selling assets.

SEEK PROFESSIONAL COUNSEL

If you're new to investing or have complex financial demands, think about getting professional counsel from a financial planner or investment professional. A financial advisor can assist you in managing shifting market conditions, creating a customized investment plan, and optimizing your portfolio.

You may create a diverse investment portfolio that will help you reach your financial objectives and provide long-term growth by adhering to these essential guidelines and using a disciplined approach to investing. Even in times of market volatility, never forget to exercise patience, maintain long-term focus, and remain devoted to your investing approach.

CHAPTER TEN

APPROACHES TO REDUCING DEBT: PRUDENT DEBT MANAGEMENT

A prevalent aspect of many people's financial lives in the modern world is debt. Being indebted may be very stressful and burdensome, whether it be from mortgages, credit card debt, or student loans. Still, you can manage your debt and strive for financial independence if you use the appropriate techniques and attitude.

Evaluate Your Debt Conditions

Knowing exactly how much you owe is the first step towards managing your debt. List all of your debts, including with the amount owed, the interest rate, the minimum amount that must be paid each month, and the due dates. This will help you prioritize your repayment efforts and provide you with a clear picture of your financial commitments.

Make an Expense Plan

An effective tool for handling your money and setting debt repayment as a top priority is a budget. Monitor your earnings and outgoings to find opportunities for reduction and reallocate funds to debt settlement. Make sure you pay at least the minimum amount owed on all of your obligations by allocating a percentage of your monthly income towards debt repayment.

Give High-Interest Debt Priority

Not every debt is made equally. If left unchecked, high-interest debt—like credit card debt—can easily get out of control. Prioritize paying off high-interest debt early because you will ultimately pay less in interest. Take into consideration applying the "debt avalanche" strategy, which entails paying the minimal amount on other debts while focusing on the loan with the highest interest rate first.

Examine Your Options for Debt Consolidation

Consolidation of debts refers to the process of consolidating several loans into one with a reduced interest rate. In addition to perhaps saving you money on interest payments, this can also make repayment more feasible. To simplify your repayment procedure and consolidate your obligations, consider choices like home equity loans, personal loans, and balance transfer credit cards.

Talk to your creditors
Don't be afraid to contact your creditors and explain your circumstances if you are having trouble making your debt payments. A lot of creditors are open to working with you to create a repayment schedule that suits your spending capacity. This could entail negotiating a settlement amount, cutting your monthly payments, or lowering your interest rate.

Reduce Spending and Raise Revenue

Think about strategies to reduce your spending so you have more money to pay off debt. Reducing discretionary spending, relocating, or finding ways to supplement your income through freelancing or side gigs are some examples of how to do this. You'll make more headway with debt repayment if you can contribute every extra dollar.

Make Good Use of Windfalls

Refunds on taxes, bonuses, or inheritances are examples of windfalls that might greatly accelerate your debt payback. Consider utilizing windfalls to lessen your total financial load and pay off debt rather than splurging on pointless things. By doing this, you'll get closer to your debt-free status and ensure long-term financial stability.

Remain Driven and Unwavering

Debt repayment is a journey, not a sprint. Following your repayment plan takes discipline, tolerance, and tenacity, particularly in the face of obstacles or unforeseen costs. Celebrate minor accomplishments along the road, monitor your development, and picture the financial freedom you will experience when you have paid off your debts to keep yourself motivated.

Get Expert Assistance If Necessary

Do not be reluctant to seek expert assistance if you are feeling overburdened by debt or finding it difficult to go forward on your own. You can get advice and support from credit counseling organizations, financial consultants, and debt relief programs to help you manage complicated financial circumstances and create a personalized debt payback plan.

Honor Your Achievements
Lastly, remember to recognize and honor your accomplishments along the route. Reaching financial freedom is a major accomplishment that is made possible with each debt paid off. Be proud of your accomplishments and use them as inspiration to keep working toward your debt-free status.

You can take charge of your finances, lessen the amount of debt you owe, and create the foundation for a better financial future by putting these tactics into practice and adhering to your payback schedule. Recall that prudent debt management is a journey, and that each action you take to reduce your debt will get you one step closer to reaching your financial objectives.

CONCLUSSION

FINAL THOUGHTS: REACHING SIX FIGURES AND BEYOND

Congratulations for starting this life-changing path to financial achievement! You've received priceless knowledge and techniques to help you reach your goal of having a six-figure bank account as you've investigated the many aspects of wealth-building, from comprehending your financial situation to developing a prosperous attitude.

You have gained knowledge about the significance of establishing specific financial objectives, creating a customized financial plan, and gaining the self-control and flexibility required to deal with the ups and downs of your financial journey throughout this book. You now understand the importance of investing in your own education and skill-building, as well as how to generate various revenue streams and use passive income to build long-term wealth.

As you take stock of your current situation and look forward to the future, keep in mind that achieving financial success means more than just hitting a certain income target. It also means realizing financial security, freedom, and peace of mind. It's about having the means and freedom to follow your passions, provide for your loved ones, and have an independent life.

Remember these important guidelines as you proceed down your route to financial success:

Establish Specific Objectives: Clearly and precisely define your financial objectives. Having well-defined objectives serves as a road map for achieving any objective, be it debt repayment, retirement savings, or business development.

Build a Plan: Assemble a customized financial strategy that fits your priorities, values, and end objectives. Define milestones to monitor your progress, break down your goals into manageable steps, and stick to your strategy despite obstacles.

Invest in Yourself: Continue your education and personal development. You may raise your earning potential and boost your possibilities by investing in your education, talents, and personal development.

To enhance resilience and financial security, it is advisable to diversify your income by establishing numerous sources of income. Investigate a variety of revenue sources, such as side gigs and entrepreneurship, to optimize your earnings.

Cultivate Financial Discipline: Make mindful decisions and behaviors around your finances. Aim to stay within your budget, cut back on frivolous spending, and give saving and investing for the future first priority.

Remain Open-Minded and Flexible in the Face of Change: Be Adaptable, Along the process, learn from setbacks and failures and adjust to changing conditions and opportunities.

Recall the reason you started this trip in the first place by keeping your focus on your why. Make sure your goals are top of mind to stay inspired and motivated, whether they be to support your family, become financially independent, or follow your aspirations.

Recall that success is a lifetime endeavor rather than a destination as you proceed on your path to six figures and beyond. Never give up on the financial future you want; instead, remain steadfast in the face of adversity and dedicated to your goals. You can design the abundant and fulfilling life you deserve with perseverance, self-control, and a clear goal for success. Cheers to your ongoing success and well-being!

www.ingramcontent.com/pod-product-compliance
Lightning Source LLC
Chambersburg PA
CBHW070359230526
45471CB00006B/2640